FOOTBALL'S #1s!

by K. C. Kelley

SCHOLASTIC INC.

Photo Editor: Cynthia Carris

Photos ©: cover main: padnpen/Getty Images; cover grass background: PhotoAlto/
Sandro Di Carlo Darsa/Getty Images; cover lights background: winui/Shutterstock, Inc.;
back cover left: Jim McIsaac/Getty Images; back cover right: Scott Boehm/AP Images; 1,
5: mphillips007/Getty Images; 6: Jim McIsaac/Getty Images; 7: Scott Boehm/AP Images;
8: Ezra Shaw/Getty Images; 9: Andy Lyons/Getty Images; 11 top: Dan Anderson/ZUMA
Press/Newscom; 11 bottom: Ronald Martinez/Getty Images; 12 top: Tom Dahlin/Getty
Images; 12 bottom: Mike McGinnis/Getty Images; 14: Wesley Hitt/Getty Images; 15: Tim
Umphrey/AP Images; 17 top: Curtis Compton/AP Images; 17 bottom: Gary Hershorn/
AP Images; 18 top: Mark Zaleski/AP Images; 18 bottom: Al Tielemans/AP Images; 20:
Aaron Doster-USA TODAY Sports/Reuters; 21: Vinny Carchietta/ZUMA Press/Newscom;
22: Brett Carlsen/Getty Images; 23: John Minchillo/AP Images; 25 top: Kevin Terrell/AP
Images; 25 bottom: John Pyle/Cal Sport Media/Newscom; 26: Paul Jasienski/AP Images;
27: Steven Senne/AP Images; 28 top: Al Messerschmidt Archive/AP Images; 28 bottom:
Thearon W. Henderson/Getty Images; 30: David Rosenblum/Icon Sportswire DFH/David
Rosenblum/Icon Sportswire/Newscom; 31: Peter Aiken/Getty Images; 32 top left: David
Zalubowski/AP Images; 32 top right: Peter Brouillet/Getty Images; 32 bottom left: Cliff
Welch/Icon SMI 357/Newscom; 32 bottom right: Doug Pensinger/Getty Images.

978-1-338-03274-1

All rights reserved. Published by Scholastic Inc. *Publishers since 1920.*
SCHOLASTIC and associated logos are trademarks and/or registered trademarks of Scholastic Inc.

10 9 8 7 6 5 4 3 2 1   16 17 18 19 20

Designed by Cheung Tai
Printed in the U.S.A.   40
First printing, September 2016

Who's No. 1?

Who's No. 1? Every football fan thinks their team is the answer to that question. Of course, right now, the real answer is the Denver Broncos, who won Super Bowl 50 in February 2016. They defeated the Carolina Panthers, 24–10. Guess that makes the Panthers No. 2!

While it's easy to say what team is No. 1, it's a little harder to do that with players. Everyone has an opinion. Some say it's their hometown hero. Others look at the stats and come up with an answer. Still others change their minds as a new star comes out each NFL weekend.

In this book, we'll present our choices for No. 1 in lots of different ways. We broke down each of the key positions into the skills needed for NFL success. We looked at the record books, checked out the players, gazed into a crystal ball . . . and came up with our answer. (Just kidding about the crystal ball!) Basically, we chose our No. 1 for each key football skill.

Do you agree with all of them? Do you agree with any of them? Who do you think we left out? That's the best part about trying to figure out who's No. 1: It sure is fun to talk about, right?

A quarterback has one job: to lead his team to victory. So we'll start our roll call with the guy who has done more winning than any other QB in the NFL. New England's **Tom Brady** is our **NO. 1 WINNER**. Since he entered the league in 2000, he has been the starter in more wins than any other QB. His 172 career regular-season wins rank third among all signal callers in NFL history. (With 186 wins each, only Brett Favre and Peyton Manning led their teams to more victories.) The Patriots have had a winning season in each of Brady's fourteen years as a starter. Plus, he has led the team to four Super Bowl championships. That's tied with San Francisco's Joe Montana and Pittsburgh's Terry Bradshaw for the most ever!

Brady's best weapon is his passing arm. But many of today's quarterbacks also change games with their feet. One player stands out, however, as the game's **NO. 1 RUNNING QB**. Carolina's **Cam Newton** is almost as dangerous running as he is passing . . . and he's really good at that, too! In five years, Newton has scored 43 touchdowns on the ground. That's tied with Pro Football Hall of Famer Steve Young for the all-time career best by a QB . . . and Young needed fifteen seasons to reach that mark! Newton has rushed for more than 500 yards in each of his five seasons. Newton also set an NFL record for QBs with 14 rushing TDs as a rookie in 2011. In 2015, he scored 10 times on the ground while leading the Panthers to the best record in the NFL! With Newton's running skills, it's almost as if the Panthers have twelve offensive players, not just eleven.

am Newton also can pass, of course. He has 117 touchdown tosses in five seasons. But other passers have stronger arms. In fact, one of them has the mightiest arm in the game. Green Bay's **Aaron Rodgers** is our **NO. 1 STRONG ARM** among quarterbacks. Rodgers has been the Packers' QB for eight years, and he has led the league in passing twice. Five times he topped 30 touchdown passes in a season. But he's our No. 1 here for the power of his arm. He can throw the deep ball better than any other passer. Evidence? In a 2015 game against Detroit, he heaved a pass that flew almost 70 yards in the air. It was the last play of the game, and when the ball landed in teammate Richard Rodgers's hands . . . Green Bay won! All thanks to Aaron Rodgers's rocket!

Rodgers's pass landed on target, a key part of a QB's job. Another veteran passer makes the list as the **NO. 1 ACCURATE PASSER**. Down in New Orleans, some fans thought 6' 0" **Drew Brees** might not be tall enough to be a big-time NFL QB. He has proved them wrong. In fifteen seasons, he has led the league in passing yards six times. Three times he led the league in completion percentage. That means he completed a greater portion of his attempted passes than any other QB. In fact, in NFL history, Brees ranks tops among all QBs with a career completion rate of 66.4 percent. Add in a Super Bowl championship with the Saints in the 2009 season and you've got a player who really is on target . . . for the Pro Football Hall of Fame.

Quarterbacks have physical skills, for sure. They need to be strong and accurate passers. Running well helps, too. But one of the QB's key jobs is leadership. By how he acts and what he says, a QB can carry a team to victory, sometimes on desire alone. With a pair of surprising Super Bowl wins under his belt, and a reputation for quiet toughness, our **NO. 1 LEADER** is **Eli Manning** of the New York Giants. Against all the odds, Manning's cool leadership helped the Giants upset the previously undefeated Patriots to win Super Bowl XLII in the 2007 season. Four years later, Manning's Giants shocked the Patriots again in Super Bowl XLVI. While Manning has a strong arm, his real success comes from his ability to lead his team out of trouble. In the clutch, he comes through!

Finally, who puts it all together the best? Who is a winner, a leader, a runner, and a powerful, accurate passer? Our **NO. 1 ALL-AROUND QB** is Seattle's **Russell Wilson**. In 2015, he became the first NFL QB to pass for more than 4,000 yards (4,024) and more than 30 TDs (34), and run for more than 500 yards (533) in the same season. He also led the league in passer rating (110.1), which combines several passing statistics. He's a strong leader, too. In four seasons in Seattle, he has taken his team to the playoffs four times. In two of those years, the Seahawks bounced back from tough starts under his guidance. They also have reached a pair of Super Bowls, winning Super Bowl XLVIII in the 2013 season.

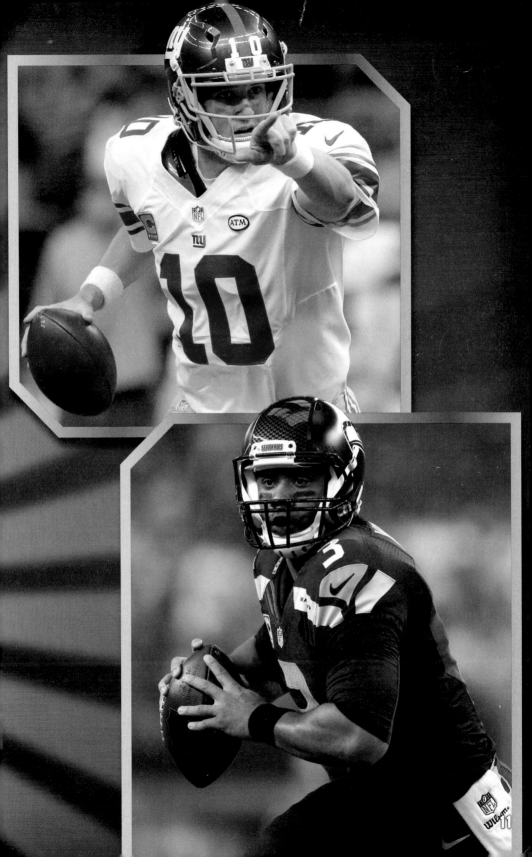

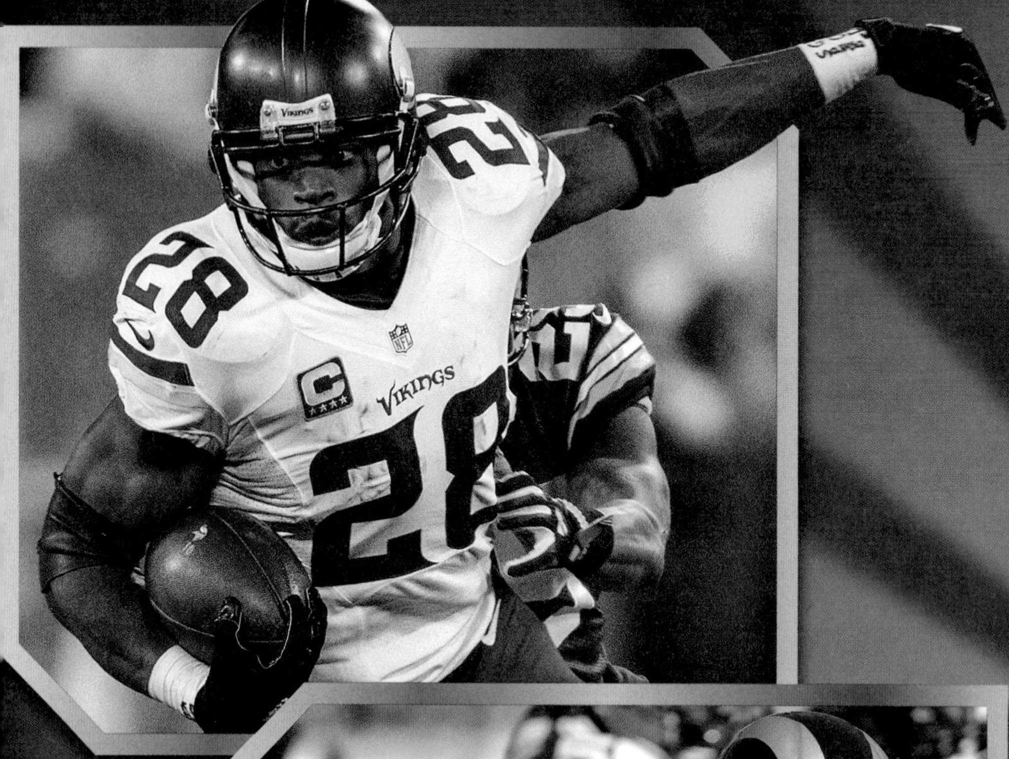
VIKINGS

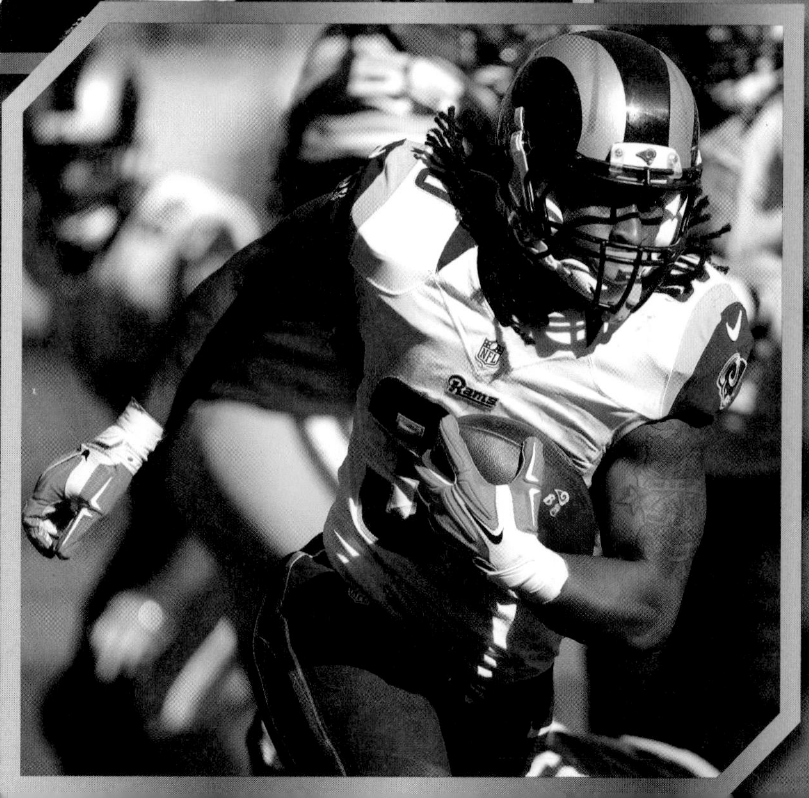
Rams

Running backs have one of the NFL's toughest jobs. They also need the game's most complete set of skills. They need to be able to do just about everything well except make tackles! Looking at a solid group of NFL runners, one stands out as the **NO. 1 ALL-AROUND** back. There's almost nothing Minnesota's **Adrian Peterson** can't do on the football field. He is tremendously fast. At a solid 217 pounds, he's a load to tackle. He can power through the middle or cut around the end and outrace safeties. Throw him the ball, and he'll find room to turn a short pass into a long gain. Peterson led the NFL in rushing yards for the third time in 2015. He gained 1,485 yards that year. His career high of 2,097 yards in 2012 was the second-highest single-season total ever! He also has scored at least 10 touchdowns in each of his eight full seasons.

Who's coming up on Peterson's heels? Several young runners might be the answer to that question. We're going with **Todd Gurley** of the Los Angeles Rams as the **NO. 1 UP-AND-COMING** star. Gurley burst onto the scene in 2015 with 125 or more rushing yards in five games, the most for a rookie since 1983. His 566 yards in his first four starts were the most ever. He scored 10 TDs and ran for a total of 1,106 yards. His reward? A trip to Hawaii after being named to the Pro Bowl in his first NFL season!

Adrian Peterson and Todd Gurley are fast, and certainly powerful. But when you need a couple of yards, you want the **NO. 1 POWER RUSHER**. That's **Eddie Lacy** of the Green Bay Packers. Take a quick look at the burly Lacy, who is listed at 234 pounds, and it might be hard to tell the difference between him and his offensive linemen. But that's without the ball. Put the ball in his hands, and he becomes a one-man wrecking crew capable of running through any defenders in his path. The Packers drafted Lacy in the second round in 2013, and he scored 11 touchdowns as a rookie. He added 13 total touchdowns in 2014, when he topped 1,000 yards rushing for the second consecutive season. He dropped off a bit in 2015 but vows to come back even stronger. Like all the best power backs, Lacy has an ability to keep churning his legs even as tacklers bounce off him. When he works up a head of steam, watch out!

While Lacy mows down would-be tacklers, **Jamaal Charles** just makes 'em miss. The Kansas City Chiefs runner has the **NO. 1 MOVES**. Though he missed most of 2015 with an injury, Charles is second on the NFL's all-time list with an average of 5.5 yards per rush. He gets those yards with a hip-swiveling style and very quick feet. NFL.com once called him "the greatest open-field runner of his generation." Charles seems to glide into holes, then burst out. Once he's in the secondary, good luck to any defensive back who tries to tackle him. By the time the defender gets there, Charles will be somewhere else!

While Eddie Lacy pounds and Jamaal Charles swerves, other backs catch. The use of running backs in the passing game is a key part of many offenses. Becoming a two-way threat is a great way to earn a regular spot in any lineup. In 2015, Atlanta's **Devonta Freeman** got a surprise chance to start. He made the most of it. His great hands and speed after the catch make him our **NO. 1 PASS-CATCHING BACK**. Freeman's 73 catches in only his second NFL season ranked third among NFL running backs in 2015. But it was his two-way ability that set him apart. He caught 3 touchdown passes, and he also tied for the NFL lead with 11 rushing scores. Look for him to put up big fantasy football numbers in 2016.

Finally, it's time to hit the goal line. In many games, the result comes down to one player battling through a ton or so of players to fight his way into the end zone. Often, this is a power back who gets the ball with one job to do—cross the goal line! **Chris Ivory** of the New York Jets gets the nod as the **NO. 1 GOAL-LINE BACK**. In 2015, 5 of his career-high 7 rushing scores were from 3 yards or closer. Ivory had his best season in 2015 with 1,070 yards. He earned many of them the hard way: a few at a time in the face of tough defenses.

n recent years, the NFL has become pass happy. Offenses are relying on receivers more than ever before. Every team has a handful of speedy, reliable, courageous pass catchers. There's a lot of talent at the position of wide receiver.

Two players, however, set themselves apart from the pack in 2015. That's why we have a tie for **NO. 1 ALL-AROUND RECEIVER**. **Julio Jones** of the Atlanta Falcons and **Antonio Brown** of the Pittsburgh Steelers are so similar, it's almost impossible to choose one over the other. Before 2015, no NFL player ever had at least 135 catches and 1,800 receiving yards in the same season. After 2015, two had: Jones (136 catches and 1,871 yards) and Brown (136 catches and 1,834 yards).

Both players have all the skills a receiver needs: great hands, speed, moves, and courage. Jones, who played his fifth season in 2015, is a little better on longer passes down the field than Brown (but not by much). His quickness helps him separate from defenders. Brown, a six-year veteran, makes more of his catches going across the middle. That's a dangerous area, as defenders can zero in on the pass catcher while he waits for the ball. In fact, Brown was knocked out in a playoff game while going after a pass over the middle. Catching passes in the NFL is not easy!

What both players share is their quarterback's trust. Atlanta and Pittsburgh QBs know that they always have a super pass-catching target when these two players are on the field.

Few plays are as exciting as a long pass. The wide receiver streaks down the field. The ball arcs high overhead. Ball and receiver meet, and what happens? Well, that depends on the receiver! Many NFL pass catchers are great at snagging the long ball. However, just one wins the title here as the **NO. 1 DOWNFIELD RECEIVER**. Cincinnati's **A. J. Green** is a five-time Pro Bowl selection in large part because of his defense-stretching speed. He gets downfield under his quarterback's passes better than anyone else. He has at least one touchdown of 80-plus yards in each of his last three seasons. He has averaged nearly 15 yards per catch since joining the Bengals in 2011 as a first-round draft pick. Next time you watch the Bengals play, keep an eye out for Green where you see the most green!

All receivers have hands, of course. But in the NFL, "hands" means more than just having a place to put your gloves. It means having the ability to catch anything, anywhere. One young player is head, hands, and shoulders above the rest as owning the **NO. 1 HANDS**. The New York Giants' **Odell Beckham Jr.** lit up social media in 2014 with one particular catch. What a catch it was! He leaped backward and, with just three fingers of one hand, reached to snag the ball before falling over a Dallas defender for a big TD. The second-year player in 2015 has a career's worth of highlight catches already. No other player ever put up more receiving yards in his first 16 NFL games than Beckham. He has 25 TDs and 2,755 yards in just two seasons. Every time Beckham takes the field, camera operators get ready—they might have to "catch" something special, too!

When footballs fly through the air, someone has to go up and get them. Quarterbacks aren't perfect, and sometimes that ball zips a little higher than they want it to. That's when they depend on high-flying receivers. The **NO. 1 RECEIVER IN THE AIR** is **DeAndre Hopkins** of the Houston Texans. His leaping skills put the "hop" in his last name. Only 6' 1", he has the leaping ability of a basketball star. He is able to climb over defenders to get the ball. Hopkins is not all "air balls," however. In 2015, his third NFL season, he really came into his own. He snagged 111 catches, including 11 for touchdowns, and racked up 1,521 receiving yards. That last number was the most in Texans history, making him No. 1 in another category!

Finally, you can't talk about NFL receivers without mentioning tight ends. That position has become one of the most important on the field. Several players have reinvented the tight end job with their great size and skill. The **NO. 1 TIGHT END**, though, is an easy pick. **Rob Gronkowski** of the New England Patriots set an NFL record for his position with 17 TDs in 2011. He's the first tight end ever with five seasons of 10 or more touchdowns, and he has made it to four Pro Bowls. When the 6' 6", 265-pound Gronk wants the ball, he's almost impossible to stop. After he makes the catch, he becomes the biggest runner in the league, knocking over defenders left and right on his way to the end zone.

So far, we've looked at offensive players. Now it's the defense's turn. Who are the No. 1 players at key defensive skills?

One of the most exciting plays in football (as long as you're not a quarterback!) is the sack. And no one sacks the quarterback better than the **NO. 1 PASS-RUSHER**, **J. J. Watt** of the Houston Texans. Watt has a tremendous "motor." That means he never stops moving. His combination of size (6' 6", 290 lbs.), speed, and drive makes him almost unstoppable. Watt's long arms also cause problems for QBs because he is great at knocking down passes. In 2012, 2014, and 2015 he was named the NFL Defensive Player of the Year. He led the NFL with 20.5 sacks in 2012 and with 17.5 sacks in 2015. When he's not crushing QBs, he plays a little offense, too. He has caught 3 touchdown passes while lining up in short-yardage situations!

Not every tackle is a sack, of course. When the ball carrier is on the loose, it's often the hard-nosed linebackers who come up to make the stop. Right now, the **NO. 1 TACKLER** is linebacker **NaVorro Bowman** of the San Francisco 49ers. He topped the NFL with 154 tackles in 2015. How tough is Bowman? He did that after missing all of the 2014 season with a knee injury. Bowman has a nose for the ball. His specialty is attacking the opponent's rushing game, but he can get after the passer, too: He has 11.5 career sacks. Bowman has been an all-pro selection every full season he has played since 2011.

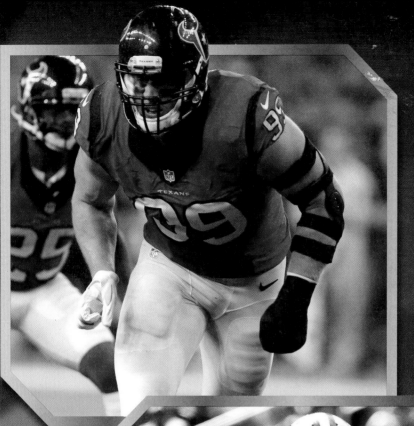

huge part of defense is shutting down powerful
passing offenses. The secondary does that by covering
receivers . . . or by taking away the ball! Sticking
like glue to the NFL's fastest receivers is a tough job.
er does it well enough to be the **NO. 1 COVER**
ER. Seattle Seahawks cornerback **Richard Sherman**
attitude that says, "No one catches anything!" He
s football smarts with great speed and toughness.
n spends hours studying video of opponents. He puts all
y into action on the field. Opponents often put together a
void his side of the field. That makes him valuable to his
en if he doesn't break up a single pass! In fact, he led the
n 8 interceptions in 2013. Since then, he has picked off
asses in two seasons. Why? Few quarterbacks dare to
e him now!

When it comes to interceptions, a lot of defensive backs are in the mix for the top spot. Why so many? After offenses discover that a player is a fierce ball hawk, they often stop throwing the ball his way! In fact, you have to go back to 1982 to find a player who led the NFL in interceptions in back-to-back years (Everson Walls, Dallas). So for the **NO. 1 INTERCEPTOR**, we'll go with the hot hand. Rookie cornerback **Marcus Peters** of the Kansas City Chiefs tied for the NFL lead in 2015 with 8 picks. Plus, he carried 2 of those interceptions back for scores, also to lead the league. Peters's stellar defense helped the Chiefs put together a 10-game winning streak that carried them to the playoffs. Peters was also selected for the Pro Bowl. Expect more great seasons from Peters . . . if not interceptions!

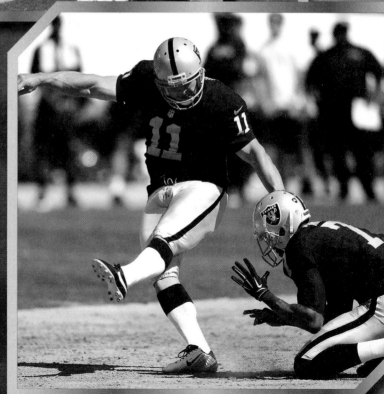

ffense and defense get most of the attention in the NFL. The other third of the game, however, can be almost as important. Special teams often are the key to victory ... or the reason for a defeat. Here are some of the No. 1 stars on special teams.

Kickers contribute hundreds of points to NFL offenses each year. They aren't the big, bad, powerful players who do most of the work. But their talent often makes all that work pay off. They need to be accurate and dependable. In that area, **Stephen Gostkowski** of the New England Patriots is the **NO. 1 SCORING KICKER**. It helps that he's in a high-powered offense, but he almost always comes through. He ranks third in NFL history in field-goal accuracy. Three times he has led the league in field goals made. He has also scored more points than any other player five times, including every season since 2012. And you want clutch? In 2015, he hit a 54-yard kick with one second left to give New England a victory over the New York Giants.

Gostkowski made that long kick, but there is another kicker with an even stronger leg. **Sebastian Janikowski** of Oakland is the **NO. 1 LONG-DISTANCE KICKER**. In 2000, the Raiders made Janikowski only the third kicker ever chosen in the first round of the NFL Draft. In the sixteen seasons since, he has made an amazing 56 percent of his attempts from 50 yards or farther. He has at least one field goal of 50-plus yards in every season except one. His 52 total field goals of 50-plus yards are tied for the most in NFL history. He was the first NFL kicker with two 60-yard kicks. One of those tied the then-NFL record of 63 yards in 2011. That's a leg!

pecial teams can score on field goals, but they also can return kicks for scores. When it comes to that job, the **NO. 1 RETURN MAN** is not just for right now . . . but for all time! Atlanta's **Devin Hester** has returned 14 punts for touchdowns. That's the most in NFL history by 4 scores! Add in 5 kickoff-return TDs, and he's No. 1 in the all-return category, too. Few players in history have led the NFL in both punt-return average and kickoff-return yards. Hester has three titles in the first and two in the second. He helped the Bears reach Super Bowl XLI in the 2006 season. He electrified the crowd by returning the game's opening kickoff 92 yards to the house! No one does it better than this ten-year veteran.

Someone has to kick all those balls to Hester and his return mates. Punters need a combination of power, timing, good hands, and guts. They face a determined rush and have to make pinpoint kicks. They can't let wind, rain, or giant defenders stop them. It's harder than it looks! The **NO. 1 ALL-AROUND PUNTER** can do all those things and more.

Dustin Colquitt of Kansas City comes from a punting family. His dad, Craig, was an NFL punter for seven years. His brother, Britton, punts for the Denver Broncos. Dustin, who played his eleventh NFL season in 2015, has perfected his special craft. Not only can he boom the ball for distance, but he also has become an expert at placing the ball inside the opponent's 20-yard line. He uses a special kick that comes from rugby. By holding the ball at different angles, or kicking it with different parts of his foot, he can make it bounce (almost) whatever way he wants. When the Chiefs need a lift, Colquitt can provide it . . . by getting a good bounce!

▷ NFL rules say that only the following positions can wear jerseys with the number 1: quarterback, punter, and kicker.

A long with Cam Newton of the Panthers, here are some of the most successful NFL players who wore a jersey with . . . the number 1!

Warren Moon

Beginning in 1984, he played seventeen NFL seasons at quarterback, mostly for the Houston Oilers . . . the strong-armed passer had already been a star in the Canadian Football League . . . twice led the NFL in passing yards . . . named to nine Pro Bowls . . . elected to the Pro Football Hall of Fame in 2006.

Jason Elam

This kicker made 436 field goals in seventeen seasons, mostly with Denver, from 1993 to 2009 . . . tied the then-NFL record with a 63-yard field goal in 1998 . . . played on two Super Bowl–winning teams with the Broncos . . . made at least one field goal of 50-plus yards every year of his career. . . named to three Pro Bowls.

Reggie Roby

A punter with a powerful leg, he played for 16 seasons (1983–1998), most of them with the Miami Dolphins . . . wore several numbers during his career, including number 1 while with the Washington Redskins in 1993 and 1994, and while with the Tampa Bay Buccaneers in 1995.

Gary Anderson

Kicked for twenty-three seasons (1982–2004), including thirteen with the Pittsburgh Steelers . . . ranks second in NFL history with 538 career field goals . . . while with Minnesota in 1998, was perfect during the regular season, making all 35 field goals and all 59 extra-point attempts . . . named to the Pro Bowl four times.